D0948981

# A Book Is Just Like You!

## All About the Parts of a Book

Kathleen Fox

Illustrations by John Wallace

**UpstartBooks**

Madison, Wisconsin
www.upstartbooks.com

To every part of a book.
You are all important.

**K.F.**


For Harry

**J.W.**

WARNING!

You'll never look at
a book the same way
again after reading
this one.

Published by UpstartBooks
4810 Forest Run Road
Madison, Wisconsin 53704
1-800-448-4887

Text © 2012 by Kathleen Fox
Illustrations © 2012 by John Wallace
The paper used in this publication meets the minimum requirements of American National
Standard for Information Science — Permanence of Paper for Printed Library Material.
ANSI/NISO Z39.48.

# Table of Contents

On the day you were born, you were given a name.

A book is given a name, too. Its name is called a TITLE.

# Just like you have a family…

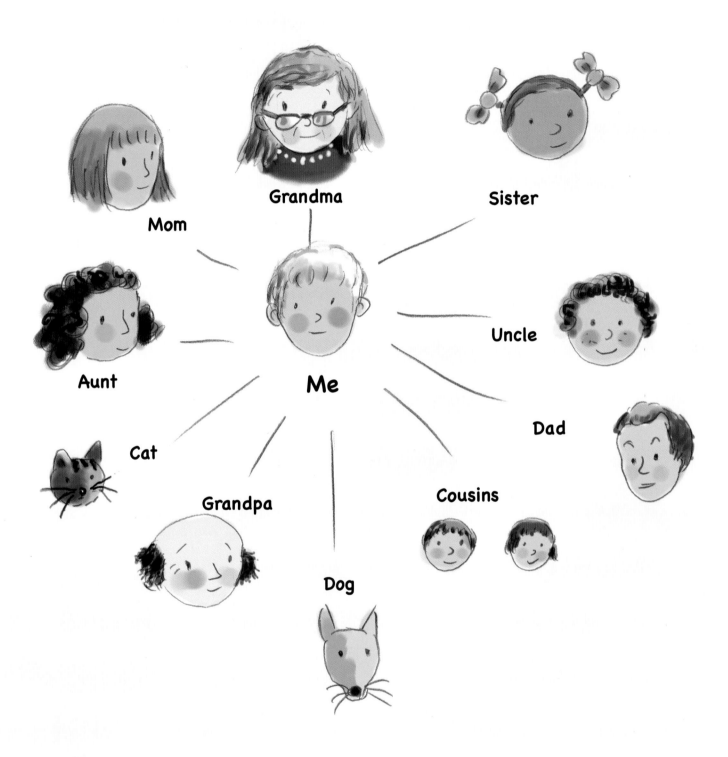

… A book has a family, too. The AUTHOR writes the book, the ILLUSTRATOR creates the pictures, the EDITOR checks the book over to get it ready to publish, the DESIGNER puts the words and pictures onto the pages, and the PUBLISHER helps everyone put the book together.

I write the story.

**Author**

I revise the work.

**Editor**

I create the pictures.

**Illustrator**

I make it look good.

**Designer**

I put it all together.

**Publisher**

Just like you celebrate a birthday…

...a book has a birthday, too. It's called a COPYRIGHT DATE. It is the day the story officially becomes a book.

By the way, where were you born?

Just like you, a book was born somewhere.
Its birthplace is called the PLACE OF PUBLICATION.

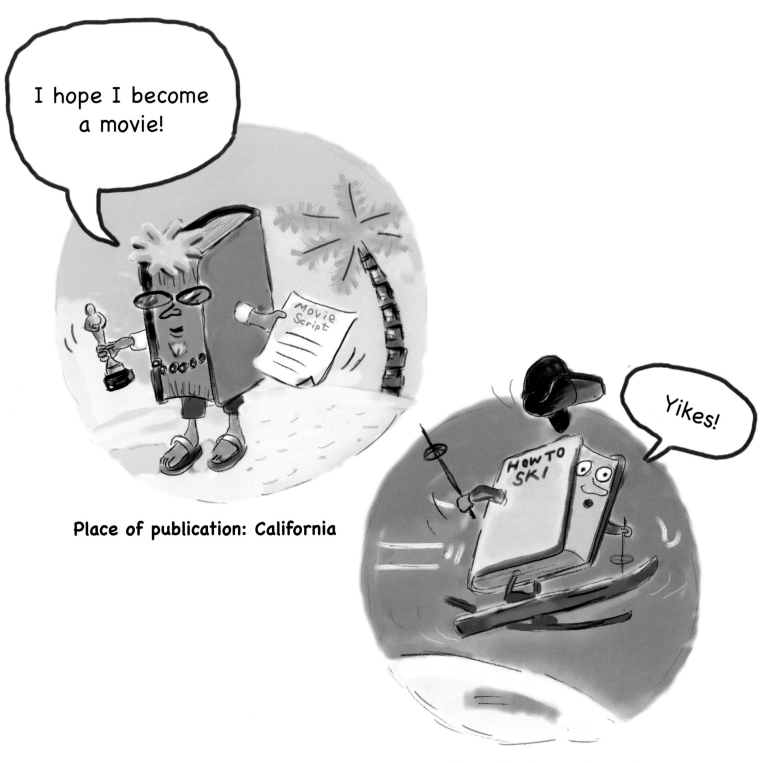

Place of publication: California

Place of publication: Wisconsin

What's another name for your pointer finger? Sometimes it's called an index finger. By using it, you point people to where something can be found. That index finger of yours has probably pointed to cookies in the grocery store you hope your mom might buy. Using your index finger is direct and fast.

A book has an INDEX, but it's not a finger. It is a special section that lists subjects in alphabetical order, and it gives you their page numbers. A book's index points you in the right direction so you can find what you need, fast.

INDEX

| | |
|---|---|
| Chicken | 7 |
| Chilli | 13 |
| Chinese Food | 39 |
| Chips, potato | 45 |
| Chips, tortilla | 9 |
| Chocolate | 11 |
| Cocoa | 15 |
| Coffee | 59 |
| Cookies | 7, 55, 93–102, 105–121, 129 |

Sometimes when you open your mouth, things come out. No, not yawns, silly—words! Words help you say what you're thinking or feeling. They are an important way to express yourself.

A book does the same. It expresses itself to the reader by using TEXT. Text is just a fancy word for the language in a book.

The way a book speaks is through its text and illustrations.

Do you ever feel like going to school naked? Don't do it! You wear clothes to keep warm, protect your skin, show off your fashion sense and, of course, to keep out of the principal's office.

Books wear clothes, too. Book clothing is called a COVER, or JACKET, and like clothes, it keeps the inside of a book protected from things like … oh, crazy kids with sticky ice-cream fingers and little baby brothers.

When you were little, you learned your address just in case you ever got lost, right? Getting lost is a pretty scary thing, but if you know your address, then a friend can get you home safely.

Believe it or not, a book has an address too. The CALL NUMBER on a book is its address in the library.

Stretch your arms behind your body and touch your back. Do you feel that knobby line going up the middle? It's called your spine, and it helps to keep your body together.

A book has a SPINE, too! It's that long bit on the outside where the covers meet. It's not as bumpy as yours, but it keeps the book's body of pages all together. It also displays the title and author's name, so the book can easily be found on a shelf.

Are there people in your life who cheer you on, like your family, friends, teachers, and coaches? Just think of everyone who has helped you accomplish the things that make you an incredibly cool kid. Whoa, you'd better start thanking those folks today!

The DEDICATION in a book usually thanks all the awesome people or organizations that helped bring the book to life. The dedication can also honor a special person in the author's life.

Where do you keep your clothes? If you said "closet," or "not stuffed under the bed," that's a good thing. When you pick out what you want to wear in the morning, you usually go to a dresser or closet. Your clothes are probably organized in that closet. Pants, here. Shirts, there. Underwear folded nicely in the top drawer. That way, you don't go to school wearing socks on your ears and hats on your feet.

A book's TABLE OF CONTENTS is kind of like an organized closet. It's the page that shows you where different sections and ideas are located.

Hey look, page 21 is about us!

Do you know someone who uses really mountainous words?
(Mountainous is a snazzy word for big.)

Sometimes a book's text uses fancy words, too. When that happens, the words may appear in bold letters. A book's GLOSSARY can tell you what those bold-lettered words mean. A glossary is like having your very own dictionary in the back of the book.

Don't gloss over the glossary!

Glossary

**mountainous:** having many mountains, huge

**saunter:** walk slowly, stroll

**institution:** organization founded for a particular purpose; place for the promotion of science, education.

**exuberance:** lively, high spirited

Did you say cookie?

Love to Bake

That glossary is one smart cookie.

The people you know, the books you read, the television you watch, the Internet you use—these can all teach you new things. When you talk about something you've learned, you usually explain where you got that information. You might say, "My teacher said…" or "I read online…" or "I heard on the radio…" When you share the source of the information, your words become more believable.

When an author borrows someone else's idea or repeats something new he's learned, he must make a list of where he got his information. That list is called a BIBLIOGRAPHY, and it's found in the back of the book. It can list other books, websites, songs, scientific stuff, quotes, history—any information the author researched and put in the book should be included in the bibliography.

How do you know so much? Everyone, every place—all that stuff?

Oh, I have my sources.

BIBLIOGRAPHY

Bibb, Kate. Using a Bibliography. New York: Hercules Press, 2011.

Jez, Allie. "Site vs. Cite." Taloo Times. March, 2000, Vol.10, p. 9.

Lesniak, Steve. Research Is A Snap. England: Celadon Press, 2010.

If it didn't come from your brain, you better put it in the bibliography.

As you can see, from title to glossary, and text to bibliography, one thing will always be true: The parts of a book are just like you!

| You | Book |
|---|---|
| Name | Title |
| Family | Author, Illustrator, Editor, Publisher |
| Birthday | Copyright Date |
| Place of Birth | Place of Publication |
| Pointer Finger | Index |
| Your Words | Text |
| Your Clothes | The Cover |
| Address | Call Number |
| Spine | Spine |
| Thanks | Dedication |
| Closet | Table of Contents |
| New Words | Glossary |
| Sharing a Source of Information | Bibliography |

# GLOSSARY

**Author:** The person who wrote the book.

**Bibliography:** Found in the back of the book, it lists sources used for research.

**Call Number:** The numbers and letters used to identify a book in the library.

**Copyright Date:** The date a book was published.

**Cover (or Jacket):** The outside part of a book that protects the inside pages.

**Dedication:** A message from the author expressing appreciation.

**Editor:** A person who improves the book and helps to get it ready to publish.

**Glossary:** A list of unique or new words and their definitions found in the back of the book.

**Illustrator:** The person who creates the images for a story.

**Index:** Alphabetical list of topics and their page numbers, usually found at the back of the book.

**Place of Publication:** The city, state, or country where the book was published.

**Publisher:** The company that prints (publishes) the book.

**Spine:** The part of the book you see when it's on the shelf. It also keeps all the pages together.

**Table of Contents:** Lists the sections in a book and their page numbers.

**Text:** The words of a book.

**Title:** The name of a book.